# ONE HUNDRED FLARF-KU

*by*

*C.P.Harrison*

A Saturn Fence Publication

Cover design and concept by Aidan Paul at Monk House

in Association with Poo Doo Photography & Design,

Austin, Texas. 2014

*for Shana*

# INTRODUCTION

Let's say….

…several years ago I found myself, as a writer, at what I thought was an intersection, a crossroads maybe, worst case scenario, one of those Irish roundabouts. Words were my spiritualism and Haiku had become my practice (after accepting that I was indeed, but a poet, never to be a novelist. A tenet I have since renounced, reclaimed and again renounced.) I was drawn to the brevity of Haiku. Boiling it all down to the essence, the bareness; Poetry at its poetry-est. I studied Haiku. The Japanese masters, the mid-century Western Revivalists, from Basho and Issa to Blyth and Higginson. I enjoyed the art of Haiku as much as the mindset, the manner in which the world seemed to appear when seeking the small moments, the tiny truths. Once I was a comfortable enough to be rejected by strangers via email, I began to submit my work to every Haiku journal and outlet I could find.

In no time at all I found myself bound and limited by this craft that had promised such freedom. The "rules" of Haiku (espoused by the self-ordained keepers of this secret order) became too confining. And not just the supposed 5/7/5 crap taught in Sophomore English Classes. Haiku, it is taught, must be directly observed in present-tense, contain a seasonal reference, a cutting word, an "a-ha moment," that while unique is recognizable, while being brief, taking no more time than the average breath as the poet demonstrates that while he is keen, he is not so clever that you'd want to cover him in fire ants as he slept.

Amid this frustration, Flarf came to the surface. Historically, Flarf began as a goof. A kind of reactive and well deserved con on the "pay to publish"-ers whose adverts run so rampant in the back of poetry periodicals and the type of digest that focuses on readers. It was language (and therefore poetry), at its most base. An art form using the everyday language and gibberish of a society facing its post-modernism (typically via the internet) to hold up a mirror to a photograph of a mirror, so to speak. The purest cut of nonsense, at once familiar but oddball, hilarious and juvenile, at times both deep and offensive. Flarf is to Found Poetry as Noah is to Ark…no, wait, COME BACK! Lines from a spam email co-mingle with craigslist pleas and website click bait to form a new literary form. As a natural collage-ist, I reveled in the idea - *It's all been said and I will use your words against you.* I scoured the web, chatrooms and bulletin boards to get my fill of flarfy freedom. (By this time there was much to be found as, with most "movements" or "scenes", by the time it "comes to the surface" it is long over.)

At the end of the hall of Flarf I found there was no end. This freedom had the freedom of endlessness, to turn back on its own tale and like the phoenix get too close to the sun and burn its paper wings. [This reference may not be accurate.] The joy in the words of anonymous internet creepers (you & I included), can unsurprisingly wear thin.

So you can see where this is going, egg before the cart and all. What if I used the boundaries of Haiku to reel in Flarf? A form where nice nibblets of nonsense are wrangled into a predictable format. Of course I was not the first to think of this, in fact I will credit Rod Smith for coining the term "flarf-ku", and though someone certainly may have termed it such prior to Smith's 2006 piece titled *flarf-ku*, it was there that I initially found and settled on the term and its format. (It could just as easily be *Flarf Ku, Flarfku, Hai-flarf,* or *Tate's Tambourine*, but Rod Smith's was the earliest mention I could locate and….tie goes to the runner?)

In 2010 & 2011, I wrote gobs of flarf-ku and eventually inundated the web with way more than my fair share.(Apology accepted.) The following is not only much of it, but also many that have sat alone until now.

*C.P.Harrison*

*2014*

# ON METHOD & THAT

Over the years, several writer friends have asked how I go
about creating flarf-ku. To be sure there are endless ways
by which it can be done. It is in no way difficult and can be
done by anyone with the want and the time to kill. (Flarf in
general and flarf-ku specifically, is akin to collage; its 1 part
the images you are lucky enough to find and 1 part how
you arrange them.)

Knowing that I wanted the pieces to at least be "of a kind"
to one another and (as I've mentioned) wanting to regulate
flarf, I decided on a couple of guidelines and rules to try to
stick with:

- each poem should have what's thought of as the
  mandatory 5/7/5 syllables of haiku (First line 5
  syllables, Second line 7 syllables, Third line 5
  syllables)
- each line should "come from" a separate source
- the words in each line should appear in order and
  verbatim, as discovered (misspellings, CAP LOCKS
  and all)

Typically I would take a series of unrelated words or
phrases, run them through an internet search engine and
think of a couple of numbers, just whatever came to mind.

For example, I'd take the words "Monday Saber-toothed Lighthouse ", enter them in Google and think 8, 4. I then would go to the 8th page of the search results, find the 4th thing returned in the results of that page and search for the best line. Generally this is just a jumping on point to get the ball on the court. I use the "two numbers method" to try to take me out of the equation, so to speak. To me the beauty lies in the randomness of the piece. Let's say the 4th result on page 8 is a review of a French film and contains the line "and the carnies dance the night away." If I choose to use this line I then have to decide how; which line is it? Do I want the 5 syllables of "carnies dance the night", do I want the 7 in carnies dance the night away," or some other variant? Not sure why but I often start with the middle 7th syllable line. Maybe because it gives me a place to "build around," but I'm not sure and it's not important. Of course 95% of the time, the 4th result on page 8 of our example, gives me nothing of interest, so I just scroll down the page and seek something I feel is better or, I pick two numbers and keep going.

One of the challenges I found with flarf-ku is the editing. I like the filth and the fury, but can find it difficult to leave bile in a poem. I have no issue with profanity, in fact, I'm a big fan, however, I don't especially want my name or poetry associated with the hateful, racist, sexist intolerant feces that the conveniently anonymous can safely sling at one another online. This fecal verbiage though, is honest, in that it is honestly what we say (again) from the anonymous comfort of our cages. It is often this off-putting language of hate, that is not only hilarious to our inner-juvenile delinquent, but when taken out of context, delivered randomly and plopped in the middle of the meaningless that it says the most, at least the most about "us." Not only is it good potty humor, but every so often it reads as the social commentary of the grand satires. That being said, there are lines & phrases I have deleted regardless of how many ways I could justify them to myself. (Again- 1 part how you arrange them.)

Despite my will to wrangle, self-monitor and design my own rules and guidelines, there are still plenty of times when I ignore my own rules. Sometimes I fine the last line just one syllable from perfect or I find it worthwhile to use a word by which I am most offended. None of this is written in stone. I encourage you to D.I.Y. Set you own rules to ignore.

As punk pioneers the Big Boys said, "...*go start your own band!*"

# ONE HUNDRED FLARF-KU

*Then again, Lionel Richie*

I.

"A wise girl kills birds
but a hungry panda throws
so simple a phrase"

II.

monday muse around
the way this poem turned out
i don't feel so good

## III.

i don't mind moby
but i can't stand moby dick...
and oh, i like dick

IV.


($11)
do not expect privacy
retaliation

# V.

I don't do drugs, I'm
a baller on QVC-
*As Seen on T.V.*

# VI.

suffer silently
to war against the problem-
we are 0 for 2

# VII.

## SCREAMING "FUCK HEAD, THERE'S SOMEONE AT THE DOOR FOR YOU!"

- this is halloween.

VIII.

What you need now is
to let go of everyone &
take me for a fool

IX.

the private world is
about half to one third long as
all the internet

X.

opportunity-
He has a penis. That's all
"you better cash-in"

## XI.

God... what have I done?

did a little crying, but

no stopping for lunch

XII.

kindly consider:
You laugh that you may not cry
into a Care Bear

## XIII.

a wee too close to
real, real fake and real stupid?
-read, that works for me

# XIV.

Remember Martin
Luther King Jr. With
20% Off

# XV.

As poet/scholar,
dude writes about everything -
it just doesn't pay

## XVI.

A ballpoint oyster!
those dumb ass Republicans,
work at making laws

## XVII.

In Australia,
wank in front of the webcam -
you've got no arms left!

# XVIII.

drink the night away-
Happy Thanksgiving sweetheart
(don't be a dumbfuck)

## XIX.

chronic bedtime
helped hammer home the message
DRUG LACED TOYZ PLEASE

## XX.

your home could use a
irregular amount of
pools - where the shrimp live

## XXI.

I could google it...
is that cat shit on the drapes?
Oh Lord, have mercy.

# XXII.

how much you indulged
The Boy with the Helium Head-
The boy can't help it!

## XXIII.

God of our fathers
you agree with everything
and all the Jesus

# XXIV.

stupid Pringles ad
some sort of "super awful"-
I just don't like it

# XXV.

**GOD IS EVERYTHING
YOU SANTIC BITCHES HE'S THE
REASON YOUR BREATHING**

## XXVI.

Biggie Smalls is dead
and he appears to have died
poorly translated

# XXVII.

deep-seated hatred
emotional or mental
...she was fine with it

# XXVIII.

Mexico welcomes a god
who throws lightning bolts
screaming **"GOOOOAAAALLLL!"**

# XXIX.

…not in a picnic
The lowest act known to man.
//scratching at your soul

# XXX.

Easter Everywhere -
Let the groovy wave take your
Santa Claus somewhere

# XXI.

derpy, derp, derp, derp/
"WTF...? I just need some"
pickles up my butt

# XXXII.

One simple word seems
to pound you into flan and
hypnotize everyone

# XXXIII.

Prophet Mohammed
added to queue "Bin Laden
making farting noises

## XXXIV.

*"Great Balls of Fire"*
yeah, they got nice ones up there
but it's not painless

# XXXV.

and for some reason,
(aka Cincinnati)
there is a "Tom Cruise"

## XXXVI.

In the summertime,
*"ding-dong, ding-dong"* all day long
—-your viewing pleasure!

## XXXVII.

Without proof, where is

The little piggy in the

"trash bag" with "douche bag"

# XXXVIII.

The laser is a laser -
facing less opposition
than most others will

# XXXIX.

The Media's Feel
ing Sorry for Palin After
Sexy Cocaine Book

# XL.

the Taiwan boob slap -
after about **THIRTY FIVE**
…. So, will Ambien

## XLI.

same schtick I tell all
Chicks With Steve Buscemeyes
-$25

# XLII.

Sharp dissagreement-
and why does a good Christian
"goddammtsomuch!!!!!"

# XLIII.

and To all my thugs
DO NOT EAT RAW CAKE BATTER
i missed this song man!!!l

## XLIV.

FALLING IN .... HE SAID

– All I Have To Offer You

is wet plastered head

# XLV.

working his way up
her stupid smile and long stride-
"Are you satisfied?"

# XLVI.

I could work my butt
with her active lifestyle and
earth beneath my feet!

# XLVII.

"Davy Jones is dead,"
she said shrugging, successfully
hiding her sadness

# XLVIII.

Rub onto hands and
chant "USA! USA!"
-wait til JC comes

# XLVIIV.

singing in one voice "

CHEESEBURGER CHEESEBURGERS
CHEESE

We Shall Overcome

# LIV.

Piss Like A Racehorse-
it's not funny. It's not fun.
(we called you a cab.)

## LV.

Fetal kick count chart'
Gave birth to the dead inside
(He breaks down and weeps...

## LVI.

say "honest to god",
"I don't MAKE trash, I BURN it!"
we're all fucking doomed.

# LVII.

what would he achieve?
a cool carbon fiber leg
& Cock-Sword Tattoo

## LVIII.

demon SHARK JUMPING-
it makes us tons of money,
although, watch out

# LIX.

like weird, like german
She Feels Successful Children
-It feels like tension

## LX.

"Is that how you'd say
leading the mother-fucker
to teaching English …

# LXI.

hardly evidence,
I gotta get my jerk on
aka Snuggie

# LXII.

Motherfucker, her
shorts were creepin up the front
- *3rd World Birdwatching*

## LXIII.

in the land of the
reblog, the insomniac
is king

# LXIV.

it was hard-hitting,
silly excuses, to squeeze
my mammoth penis

## LXV.

intercourse during
72 hours of
spilling his/

# LXVI.

it's Valentime's Day-
I'm reading Othello and
bitches still get, killed

# LXVII.

oh real-time robot
oh why, can't everything be
Super-Deformed art

LXVIII.


getting into kitsch
every dish, cup, bowl in my
Bed Bath and Beyond

## LXIX.

Like a tween, I got
but…I enjoy nut shots,
hobbling all over

# LXX.

This Mechanicle Pencil
£645
Poet: It's broken

## LXXI.

thinkin' I'm lonely-

but I've got six good friends and

all these f-ing birds

# ACKNOWLEDGMENTS

I would like to acknowledge that despite the title of this book there are not actually one hundred poems in this collection. This has not, however, affected the price of this book.

I would like to acknowledge, that I have acknowledged Rod Smith for coining the term "flarf-ku."

I would like to acknowledge the great Kenneth Rexroth for artistic and design inspiration.

I would like to express sincere gratitude to Shana Harrison, my entire family, all my friends, colleagues and every one at Saturn Fence for the inspiration, love and kindness that you have shown me.

Bye!

www.ingramcontent.com/pod-product-compliance
Lightning Source LLC
Chambersburg PA
CBHW020556030426
42337CB00013B/1109